"Drew is the master of bite-sized intelligence."
> Jeff Hasselberger, President
> Hasselberger & Associates Marketing
> Philadelphia, PA

"I thought I was a marketing expert until I read this book. Drew provides straightforward, practical tips that are sure to help any business reach new heights. This is a must read for anyone associated with marketing."
> John Gumas, President
> Gumas Advertising
> San Francisco, CA

"This book offered me a dose of marketing inspiration that can easily slip away due to busy schedules and crazy deadlines. Each idea focused me on the need for marketers to think smart and respond even smarter."
> Sharon Rea, Marketing Communications Manager
> Eagle Window and Door
> Dubuque, IA

"Drew is the master. His marketing insights are thoughtful, practical and entertaining. His 'bottom line' advice has helped us and our clients grow our businesses."
> Mark Kolakoski, President
> Royal Marketing
> Grand Rapids, MI

"DON'T WRITE THIS BOOK! As a faithful reader of Drew's weekly email, I have always felt that I had a leg up on my competition. Now everyone will know my secret as to how I've turned my start-up business into an industry leader in such a short period of time. Congratulations Drew! Your insight and wisdom into the world of marketing can help every business owner (small or large) build a prosperous relationship with their employees and customers."
> Jay Brackett, Owner
> Brackett Media & Event Services
> Des Moines, IA

"This is not a book about spin, colorful photos, and tag lines rolled out in expensive marketing campaigns. It's about the transformations that occur when we dig deep into the soul of an organization. Drew connects with his reader like a wise, old friend who believes we each have a unique gift for success."

Sharon Johnson, Executive Coach
Des Moines, IA

"Being new to this marketing world, I had stacks of books that were recommended reading. Overwhelming and ugh! But it was Drew's writings that meant the most. Quick reads, fun stories, and most importantly, practical advice that WORKS."

Cheri Bustos, Director, Corporate Communications
Trinity Regional Health System
Rock Island, IL

"There's no rhetoric or esoteric marketing theory in this book. From the very first page, it's nothing but no-nonsense marketing insights that can be put into practice immediately. This is the book I will make every employee read and give every client as a gift. It's that good."

Jean Whiddon, President
Kircher Inc.
Washington, DC

99.3 Random Acts of Marketing

99.3 Random Acts of Marketing

by Drew

Innova Training & Consulting, Inc.
Des Moines, IA

Published by

Innova Training & Consulting, Inc.

2882 106th Street, Suite 200

Des Moines, IA 50322

Phone: 1.515.278.5570

Fax: 1.515.278.2245

Email: solutions@innovatraining.com

www.innovatraining.com

Printed in the U.S.A.

Editors: Debbie Kirschman and Jennifer Chiaramonte

Graphic Design: Mike Aspengren

ISBN 0-9746-8790-1

To my source of light — Kelsey.
Just remember, if a goof like Daddy
can make his dreams come true, so can you.

Table of Contents

 Acknowledgments

This could be a book unto itself. But not a one could be omitted.

To my parents. You believed in me unconditionally and told me I could achieve anything I set my sights on often enough that I grew to believe it.

To Suzy. You never doubted it would be so. In so many ways. Thank you for believing in me and in us.

To Kelsey. I know you won't understand this yet, but you are my Jiminy Crickett. You're also my greatest source of stress relief.

To my friends who lighten my load with their laughter and good company. Knowing I can count on you being there no matter what makes taking the risks so much easier.

To the many mentors and talented marketing professionals I've worked with along the way. Thanks for letting me learn from my mistakes and for giving me many second chances.

To my business partner Jana and our merry band at Erickson • McLellan. I have never been surrounded by a more remarkable group of professionals and human beings. I will never cease to be amazed at your passion and I am grateful to be among you.

To the myriad of clients I've worked with over the past 20 years. You shared many things with me, but what I value most is your trust.

To Kathy and the crew at Innova. You shared my vision from the start. Who knew tight deadlines, endless discussions about titles and covers, budgets and contracts could be so much fun? I think we made the right decision about the scented cover.

I am eternally grateful to all of you who've influenced me. You can share in any success that this book might achieve. The mistakes, on the other hand, are probably all mine.

Preface:

For most of us, the world of marketing and the marketplace is chaos. Constant change. Internal politics. CEOs who want to pull an ad because the first time it ran, no one bought a thing. Fierce competitors. New marketing gimmicks (who thought of the urinal ads?). Tight budgets. Unreasonable sales goals. Bosses who think anyone with a computer can create an effective brochure. The 3-second attention span of a Web surfer. Blah, blah, blah.

Despite all that, marketing isn't rocket science. It's common sense. It's consistency. It's staying the course. I know that sounds pretty dull, but that's what works. It's also incredibly difficult to do.

Like the world of marketing, this book is chaos too. Purposefully. Random acts of marketing. Each page contains one thought or topic. A single marketing insight. Typically, on the job we think of marketing issues in a grander scheme, as part of an overall plan or campaign. But here, you can take your time to really concentrate on each separate idea. As for the randomness? We all know that looking at things out of order sometimes brings them into sharper focus. Try reading entries casually, in random order. When there's a specific topic that has you perplexed, or you want to reread something, you'll find an index in the back.

As you read this book I hope you'll occasionally mutter an "I'll be danged" or nod your head. You'll probably also kick yourself in the pants more than once. One of my goals is to remind you of what you already know but have let slide. Consider it a gentle nudge.

Use this book. Take notes or jot down ideas on the left side of each page. I've left them blank for that very purpose. Read a passage to the sales manager who's nagging at you to change the logo or the CEO who refuses to answer a reporter who's hounding her. Share a page or two with the employees who interact with your customers every day. Take solace in it when everyone wants you to knee-jerk react to the latest volley from a competitor or kookiest gimmick. But do something. Even if it's just to pat yourself on the back for a job well done.

Thanks for sharing my passion for marketing and the people who do it well.

– Drew

Random notes:

I'm sorry, what did you say again?

Boy, are we thickheaded. And yet businesses will use a marketing message one or two times and wonder why they haven't received a response. Admit it, haven't you run an ad once and then never used it again? Or worse yet, have you pulled an ad well before its time because the results weren't instantaneous? Long after we are really sick of an ad, our target audience is just noticing it.

Consider this...

• After 1 day, we forget 46% of what we've heard.

• After 7 days, we forget 65% of what we've heard.

• After 14 days, we forget 79% of what we've heard.

I know this sounds dismal, but you can use this information to your advantage.

When a new prospect contacts you or you begin a marketing effort, make sure your audience gets told and then told again. You should "blitz 'em" with consistent messages in a variety of media. For how long? It depends on your selling cycle.

Is your product an impulse or considered purchase? Do your potential buyers know anything about you? Do you own a brand or position in the marketplace? Is this a new campaign or product?

No matter how you answer the questions, remember this—your potential customers are slow to notice you and even quicker to forget. So stay under their nose!

Random notes:

That's music to my ears!

Think those toe-tapping tunes you hear in stores and restaurants are accidental? Think again. Music has powers untold that can be harnessed for your marketing purposes.

Restauranteurs looking to get their diners to subconsciously eat more quickly are pumping loud, fast-paced music through their dining room sound systems. That means more "table turns" in a night—and more revenue.

According to the *Bulletin of the Psychonomic Society*, people chew an average of 4.4 bites per minute to fast music and only 3.8 bites per minute to a slow beat.

In fact, many restaurants have fully computerized sound systems that automatically play faster and louder songs at the times of the day when the restaurant wants to turn more tables.

Have you ever thought about how you might influence your customers with a tune or two? Would you like them to browse and shop at a leisurely pace or keep moving? Music can also influence a person's mood. Think of the music played at sporting events and how it pumps you up for the game. Do you want your clients to be soothed? Excited? Sentimental? Lonely?

Before you set the dial on a particular radio station or Muzak® system—remember the power of the subconscious mind.

Random notes:

A direct hit?

Direct mail. Some people call it junk mail. But when properly targeted, communicating one-to-one with your customers and potential customers just makes good sense. There's less competition for their attention. You can speak very specifically to their needs or wants. It's also one of the more measurable marketing tools. But most people measure it incorrectly.

The industry standard for a good response is 2%. I get asked all the time if 2% really should be considered a success. The honest answer is yes. And no. There are just too many factors. A simple percentile return rate can't accurately reflect success or failure.

Here are some of the questions you need to ask before evaluating your direct mail piece's effectiveness:

- Who did you send it to and are they the right audience?

- Have they ever heard of you or from you before?

- What did you ask the receiver to do?

- Were you just offering free information or making an announcement?

- How expensive is your product or service?

You can get 1,000 responses for free information and generate no revenue dollars. You can also generate millions of dollars in revenue with a 0.2% response. Depending on your goals either result could be a success. Or a failure.

Random notes:

6

A gift that gives back to you

Gift certificates. Perhaps they are a sign of the harried times. For the giver, they are quick and convenient. For the receiver, they're the promise of a great gift that won't need to be returned. For a retailer, they can be incredibly profitable.

Gift cards. Gift certificates. E-gift certificates. Call them what you will, but if you own a retail business—you can probably call them money in the bank! For most retailers, they're both a great marketing tool and a profit center.

Let's start with the money side. On average, 25% of gift certificates never get redeemed. That's not a bad profit margin.

And then there's the benefit of having the money up front. One Outback Steakhouse® generated more than $30,000 in gift certificates in the month before Christmas. Could you use a surge of cash now, without laying out dollars on the cost of goods before you sell the products?

In terms of a marketing tool, gift cards work wonders. It's the ultimate in word-of-mouth advertising. Most people give gift certificates to friends and family. They're endorsing your product or service—and driving traffic to your door. Why wouldn't you want to encourage your customers to spread the word for you—especially since it's free?

Want to make your gift certificates really fly out the door? Remembering the average of 25% that are never redeemed, charge only 90 or 95% of the gift certificate's face value. Imagine the hype that will generate!

Random notes:

Straight from the horse's mouth

Whether you are the butcher, the baker or the candlestick maker—people believe testimonials. And they always have. Even back in 1924, Pond's® used the endorsements of "three of the reigning queens of Europe, six princesses, titled ladies and leaders of American society" to sell Pond's Cold Cream. It worked like a charm.

Okay, so you probably cannot get the endorsement of a queen. But that doesn't mean testimonials won't work wonders for you too. Let your customers tell their stories. How you solved their problems. What it's like to do business with you.

That's what your potential customers want to know. They want reassurance that you are going to understand and meet their needs. They need to know you won't disappoint them. They want to feel good about doing business with you. And if others like you enough to say so publicly, then that's the reassurance needed to convert a potential customer to an enthusiastic buyer.

Don't wait until you're ready to create the marketing piece to solicit client feedback. Create a mechanism that actively asks for customer comments. You can also just ask your best customers if they'd mind being in a testimonial ad. In most cases, they'll be flattered. And you'll be on your way to more business.

Random notes:

yourbusiness.com?
Maybe not

In 2000, it was estimated that there were more than 2.1 billion Web pages. So imagine how many there are today. Is yours among them? Web site usage among small businesses has grown dramatically. In 1997, one in fifteen small businesses had a Web page. By the end of 2000, it was one in five. Currently, it's one in four.

Do you have a Web site? Do the statistics mean that you should? Are you missing out on sales if you aren't driving on the Internet superhighway?

Maybe. Maybe not. While the Web makes perfect sense for many businesses, it's not for everyone. The danger in something that works for most is the assumption that it will work for all.

Is your customer or potential customer base large enough to support a Web site? Are they plugged in? Are you ready to answer email inquiries? Do you have a product or service that you could sell online? What would your customer or potential customer gain by your Web presence? Do you have the time and money to keep your site fresh and up-to-date? There's nothing worse than going to someone's Web site and finding the most current press release is two years old.

Even if everyone else is getting on the train, don't get on board until you're sure it's headed in the direction you want to travel.

Random notes:

What exactly do you sell?

It doesn't matter if you are a hospital, a shoe store or a wedding DJ...everyone sells the same thing—a benefit.

People buy solutions—or benefits—not features. They only care about what your product or service can do for them. For example, a consumer doesn't care that an answering machine has the newest microchip technology. What matters to him is that the new microchip technology means he'll never lose a call and messages can be accessed from remote locations.

There's a great story about a marketing professor who brought a shovel into class. He held it up and asked his class how they'd sell it. The students pointed out the sturdiness of the handle and the sharpness of the shovel's point. The professor stopped them and said, "People do not buy shovels. They buy holes."

Look at your product or service from a client's point of view. What can it do for her? What is the benefit? Then check to make sure your marketing communications are focusing on those benefits, as opposed to the features that make the benefits possible.

Don't make your potential customers look for what's in it for them. Don't tout the shovel's features. Tell them about the holes.

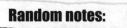

Random notes:

Speak their language

Everyone speaks their own language. Today's world is filled with acronyms, catch phrases, slang and industry jargon. It's handy to know that shorthand. But sometimes using shorthand can really mess up good marketing.

Remember this rule. Always know who you're talking to. Sounds obvious enough, doesn't it?

Unfortunately, many businesses forget that simple idea when it comes to creating marketing materials. Their brochures, Web sites and ads are filled with industry buzzwords, or the entire piece is written either above or below the intended audience reading level. Many businesses simply write in the style that is most comfortable for them, forgetting that their audience may respond to something completely different.

Next time you're creating a marketing message, stop and think about your audience. Close your eyes and hear how they would talk. Are they formal or more conversational in tone? What kinds of words do they use? What's most important to them? What kinds of questions do they ask? How do they ask them?

After you've written a draft, reread it. Look for signs that you wrote it and fix them quick! Don't let how you talk get in the way of being able to communicate.

Random notes:

A definite to-do list

The direct mail piece begs to be opened. Your agency has crafted the right message. You've got a great offer on a top-of-the-line product. And all of it could be for nothing. What you do next will probably determine the success of your efforts.

Who are you going to send your mailing to? Not putting enough time and effort into selecting the right list is probably the most common—and most fatal—error made in direct mail.

Nowadays, you can be incredibly specific when buying your list. If you want a list of men between the ages of 40 and 47 who have a bald spot, a motorcycle and size 13 feet—that list can be bought. Don't waste your money talking to people who aren't the perfect audience for your product or service. Unless the people on your mailing list need or want what you've got, they're going to be tough to convince, and probably impossible to sell.

Spend as much time and money on researching and purchasing your list as you do on the creative aspects of writing and layout. The right message to the right people.

Now that will be a direct hit!

Random notes:

You can depend on it

Accountemps® conducted a very insightful survey. They asked executives what they perceived to be the most important quality of a team player.

The top answer? Dependability when it comes to deadlines.

In today's rushed world, where emails travel the globe in seconds and sending things two-day air seems akin to the pony express, deadlines are more pressure-filled than ever. Everyone is rushing to meet a deadline for someone.

If you're a service-oriented business and you want your clients to think of you as an integral part of their team, how could you use this insight to your advantage?

What kinds of deadlines do you help your clients meet? Do your clients fret about deadlines? Do you give them reason to? How could you reassure your customer so they don't have to worry anymore? Do you have systems in place to protect important deadlines? Do you offer some sort of refund if you miss one?

Do your marketing materials address these issues? Considering how important the surveyed executives thought deadlines were... should they?

Random notes:

Who influences your customers?

In her book, *Customers.com*, Patricia Seybold tells a great marketing story of a furniture maker who specialized in day care equipment for special-needs children. He realized that although day care centers were his end buyers (they wrote the checks for his furniture), the suggestion to purchase often came from physical therapists who weren't employed by the centers.

The physical therapists influenced the sale, although they were not the buyers. Most businesses have influencers, whether the business recognizes them or not.

By targeting these influencers and making sure they knew of the benefits of his products, the furniture maker increased sales. Because an influencer has credibility with multiple prospective buyers, establishing a strong relationship with the influencer can produce a greater payoff than directly chasing the end buyers.

For an ad agency, the influencers might be media sales people or printing vendors. For an intellectual property attorney, key influencers might be corporate lawyers or college professors. For a high-end caterer, the influencers might be wine shops, interior designers or real estate agents who specialize in expensive homes.

What influencers hold the key to your customers?

Random notes:

Show them the numbers

There's often great value in telling your story using pertinent facts and figures. But just rattling off a bunch of numbers isn't enough. We've all been in presentations where the speaker showed slide after slide full of numbers. It's mind numbing.

Next time you are working on a presentation involving numbers, remember this maxim: show them rather than tell them.

Your audience will better understand the relationship between the numbers if you present the data graphically. The key to doing this with maximum effectiveness is to choose the right style of chart or graph based on the information being presented.

For maximum impact and comprehension:

- Use line charts for trends.
- Use bar charts for comparisons.
- Use pie charts for percentages.
- Use diagrams to show order and structure.

The only downside of treating numbers like this in your presentation is that you'll probably be asked to do a lot more presenting!

Random notes:

How quickly do you give up?

Maybe it's our instant gratification world, but we marketers have become an impatient bunch. Just think about it. You spent all that money and effort to develop a marketing tool, be it an ad, direct mail piece or PR campaign. You took the time to get it into the marketplace, but after the third attempt to use it, you or your CEO looked at the sales numbers and decided it just wasn't working. And you were right...it wasn't working...YET!

According to a study by Thomas Publishing Company, most marketers give up too early. The study reveals 80% of sales to businesses are made on or after the fifth contact, but only 10% of all marketing efforts go beyond three times!

When planning your marketing efforts, remember that frequency is critical to success. You have to get your customers' attention, pique their interest and create the need for your product or service. Then, you have to stay under their nose until they are ready to buy. No single ad or direct mail piece can be expected to accomplish all that in a couple of attempts.

Think of marketing as growing a garden. Plant the seeds, tend to them and with your continued patience and consistency—your garden will flourish. If you don't pull the seedling before its time!

Random notes:

Flat can be where it's at

Three-dimensional direct mail pieces are incredibly effective. But sometimes you just don't have the budget to go all out. There are still ways to help your direct mail efforts stand out in the stack of mail, even if you've decided to use a plain envelope.

Try a #11 envelope. It's slightly bigger than the standard #10 commercial envelope, so it sticks out in a crowded pile of incoming mail, and it costs the same to send. Or use some color. Of the envelopes we receive, 99% are white or some form of beige. How about trying a deep purple or tangerine? That's sure to get noticed.

Sometimes, even when a potential customer asks you to mail something to them, it can get lost in the shuffle. When prospects or clients ask for information by mail, remind them when you send it that they requested it.

Make labels made that say "Information You've Requested," and stick the label on the outside envelope or catalog. Without this label or a handwritten note that says the same thing, you risk having the recipient, or his or her gatekeeper, think your literature is junk mail.

It doesn't have to be expensive to be effective.

Random notes:

Your annual checkup

You probably thought your days of studying were long gone. Wrong. Everyone should study other businesses in their industry. Take the time to do some competitive research. For some reason, after scrutinizing a competitor's business, you see yours in a whole new light. One of the best places to do some free research on businesses that are similar to yours is by snooping through their annual reports. You'll be surprised at how much you can learn about industry trends, pricing and more.

It used to be that you'd have to be an investor or mail a request to receive a company's annual report. But thanks to the computer age, you can browse the annual report of your choice in minutes.

A great place to find more than 2,000 annual reports is www.reportgallery.com. There you will find not only annual reports, but also snapshots of the company's current and projected earnings.

If you want a hard copy of a report, check out www.annualreportservice.com. You can read thousands of annual reports online and can also request hard copies be mailed to you.

Now there's no excuse not to do your homework.

Random notes:

How much is that doggie in the window?

Pricing strategies have become a lot more sophisticated since the $9.99 versus $10.00 debate. That's because consumers have become more sophisticated too. Here are some ways to use pricing to demonstrate the real value of your product or service.

- Two-layer pricing, with regular and king-sized options. Buy the car wash or car wash with underbody spray pricing. This offer benefits the sale of both products. By differentiating the two products, buyers perceive the value of the lower-priced choice and understand that the slightly higher price gets them something extra.

- Validate a higher price by comparing your product to something shoppers know would cost them more. For instance, compare renter's insurance versus replacing apartment furniture, or checkout the cost of a will versus sorting out the estate in court.

- Sometimes you hit a ceiling in terms of pricing your product. But you can always find extra revenue for premium services like faster turnaround, bundling of products or services, extra service (like a 24-hour hotline) or on-site training.

The trick to charging more money is really about showing more value.

Random notes:

A present for me?

Let's face it, we're all kids at heart. Nothing intrigues people, young and old, more than a package addressed to them. We feel it, we shake it and try to guess its contents...but most important—we open it.

This is a beautiful thing if you are trying to get your message into the hands of a potential buyer.

Make your direct mail efforts three-dimensional. Tease the receiver into opening your package or envelope with the promise of a reward—one they can feel but can't yet see.

The gift doesn't have to be elaborate or expensive. It could be as simple as a pen, pin or magnet. Or you can go whole-hog and send something that snaps, crackles and pops when opened. You can get just about anything these days, so search for the right item that not only gets your audience's attention, but also ties to your promotion, message or image.

One of the big buzzwords today is *value added*. There's no reason why value added can't be fun added as well. You'll love the results.

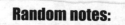

Random notes:

A pop quiz

Which of these techniques can increase readership of a newsletter, earn you coveted media coverage or boost traffic at a Web site?

a. A crossword puzzle

b. A quiz

c. A thought-provoking question

d. All of the above

The correct answer is d.

People love the opportunity to demonstrate their knowledge and test their wits. You can create custom puzzles that tie into your area of expertise. A tax consultancy got remarkable readership for its newsletter by inserting a tax-oriented quiz in each issue and offering the answers by email and on their Web site.

You can create trivia tests, true/false questions, self-scoring multiple-choice quizzes, word finds, cryptograms or crossword puzzles. Think it sounds tough? You'll find software and Web sites that make it a snap.

Random notes:

® you doing it right?

This is a definite case of better safe than sorry. Intellectual property law is a hot commodity and you don't want to be on the wrong side of a courtroom in a dispute that can easily be avoided.

Whenever you are dealing with your own company's name, a client's name or just using a trademarked company's name in your materials, always be on the safe side with trademarks.

If a name is registered, you need to indicate that with the trademark symbol (a capital R in a small circle) after the company name. The good news is that once is enough. You don't need to use a trademark symbol more than once per name per document.

By the way, did you know that you are in violation of trademark law if you use a brand name, like Kleenex® or Roller Blades® as the generic word for tissue or in-line skates? These companies are starting to take the misuse of their company or product name very seriously.

Don't get legally sideways on this one.

Random notes:

Offer expires Wednesday, March 7

There are probably very few consumers who haven't been driven to make a purchase because the sale ended "today." Why do marketers put time-dated offers in their promotions? Because they work. When consumers know they have a deadline, they can't linger on their decision too long.

In fact, it's been proven that the shorter the window of opportunity, the higher the sales. So don't have a month-long sale, make it a 12-hour one instead!

Before you give this tactic a try, make sure you are playing by the rules. Otherwise, you might find yourself in hot water with the government. The FTC has a phrase called "good faith" when it comes to time-dated sales. If you offer a one-day sale, and yet the sale keeps getting extended—you might get a review. The FTC calls that deceptive advertising.

Besides being deceptive, continuously extending the deadline sends a loud and clear message to your customers—that you say one thing and do another. Not exactly what you want them to think about your business.

Random notes:

Check it off

Ever shop at the grocery store, get home and realize you forgot one or two items? Of course! You know why, don't you? You didn't make a list.

Your clients are no different. Why not create a checklist for your customers? It's a more obvious tactic for retail establishments, but even if you sell professional services, this will work for you.

An accountant could create a list for tax preparation. How about insurance agents? They could put together an "are you protected" list. A training company that targets rising stars could offer a CEO prep list. It might look like this:

Are you ready to be CEO?

___ Team building (classes beginning in September)

___ Hiring top performers (classes beginning in January)

___ Becoming the visionary (classes beginning in March)

___ Leading through tough times (classes beginning in May)

___ Conflict resolution in the boardroom (classes beginning in July)

Sign up now for our CEO Power Pack of classes. In less than 12 months you'll be ready to take the helm!

Great idea. And something any business can offer!

Random notes:

May I interest you in another?

We all know that one of the best places to get new business is from our existing client base. But how do you go about doing that? It's not just a matter of how, but perhaps the more important question is who?

In a matter of minutes, you can create a quick grid that will give you a snapshot view of where you might be able to increase sales and profits.

Draw a box. Along the outside left-hand side of the box write the names of your current clients. Then, along the top of the box, write the products and services you offer. Draw vertical and horizontal lines within the box to separate clients and products/services. In other words, make a grid.

Starting with the first client, check off each box that corresponds to a product or service that you are currently selling to that client. Do the same for each customer you have. When you're done, look at all the empty boxes. Kind of surprising, eh?

Missed opportunities. Lost revenues. But, now that you see them—you can start checking them off!

Random notes:

A sneak preview

You've crafted a riveting press release. It has the who, the what, the where and the when. You are confident that once the assignment editor and reporter read your release, they will be compelled to give you the coverage your news deserves. Unfortunately, your release might never even get read.

Imagine it from the reporter's point of view. A reporter receives piles of releases (especially with the advent of email releases), and 90% of them aren't sent to the right reporter or might not even be newsworthy at all. So when you have a story that really does deserve some attention, how do you make sure the news media takes note?

A former editor of a regional business journal offered this insider's suggestion on getting additional news coverage.

When writing a press release, include a "why this is significant" paragraph at the beginning of the release. This should be a succinct explanation of what the release is about and why it is relevant to the person reading it.

Be careful. This is not the time to wax on. Be concise but compelling.

This sneak peek will give the reporter, editor or assignment editor enough information to entice them into reading the whole release. Many times, without a paragraph like this, if the headline doesn't grab them, the release doesn't get read.

A significance paragraph will also help you determine which reporters and media outlets should be receiving the release in the first place.

Random notes:

Oops

We all make mistakes. It might be an error on the bill. It could be a missed delivery. Or a product that doesn't live up to your guarantee. It's embarrassing. It can be costly. But it's inevitable. So, the real question is, how are you going to handle mistakes when they happen?

Too many companies adopt the ostrich mentality. They just tuck their heads in the sand and hope that no one will notice. This is never a good idea. We don't think very highly of company spokespeople who are constantly dodging questions.

Fortunately, one way to actually get into good graces with your clients/prospective clients is to admit your foibles.

Freely admit when you've made a mistake. You don't have to rent a billboard to announce it, but you shouldn't hide or deny it. Odds are the client knows it anyway. But by being up front about it, you have demonstrated how you would handle a problem — straightforward, no excuses. Your customer can rest easy—knowing that you will not try to hide, deny or ignore a problem.

You've earned their trust. And turned a potential concern into new confidence.

Random notes:

You just gotta tell them!

There is no better new business opportunity than existing customers. They have already crossed over the threshold. They've chosen to do business with you. It went well enough that they stuck around. So far so good. But right now, they've only sampled what you have to offer. You need to make sure they know the full menu!

I'm not sure if it's ignorance or arrogance, but we all think our clients know more about us than they really do. They're time-starved people, just like you. They don't have time to browse the entirety of your Web site or think about what else you might offer.

It's your responsibility to make sure they know all the different ways you can serve them.

- Bring some samples of your work for other clients to your next meeting. Take five minutes to do a little show and tell.

- Hold a "thanks for your business" cocktail party. Invite all your customers and display all of your services or products.

- Create a noticeable bill or bag stuffer that touts your products or services.

- Give them a free sample of something they've never tried.

No matter how you choose to tell them, remember they can't buy it if they don't know you sell it.

Random notes:

Red pen blues

Editing may not be your idea of a good time. Especially if it's your copy that is being edited. But, good editing takes the written word to a new level. It's about taking a critical eye and sharp pen and removing any word that does not add value. That doesn't mean your copy should be stark and sterile. It means you need to be able to justify every word.

It isn't just about cutting out words. It's also about choosing better words. Instead of saying "it was hot" try "it was sweltering." Which one helps you feel the heat?

Consistency is also a critical element of editing. Does your tone fluctuate? Do you switch between a more formal tone and a less formal one? Does it sound like the same person wrote the whole piece? Does the copy style match the graphic style and design?

When you have your editor's hat on, you also want to check sentence structure. Mix things up with complex and simple sentence combinations. If you write like I do, you can even toss in a fragment or two for emphasis!

It may not be fun. But, the results are worth the pain. If it's important enough to write, it's important enough to edit.

Random notes:

Is your cookie generic?

The state of Vermont believes, and has proven through market research, that when the general public hears the phrase "made in Vermont" they believe the product will be handmade and special. That distinction provides significant added value to Vermont's merchants. They have a valuable brand in the name of their state, so valuable that they've managed to fine companies who falsely claim their products were made in Vermont. Legal support of efforts to protect their brand equity.

So what exactly is brand equity? Imagine a generic product like a cookie. Within reason, anyone can make and sell one. There's nothing special about the product itself. In your head, decide what you'd pay for the generic cookie.

Now, imagine a specific cookie. A cookie made from a grandmother's recipe by a company known for using only natural ingredients. Every time you have bought a cookie from this company, over the past three years—it has lived up to its hype. And there's been considerable hype. How much would you pay for that cookie?

Brand equity combines brand name awareness (the hype), the level of confidence or high regard that is associated with your company or products because of your brand (the grandmother's special recipe and all natural ingredients), and the loyalty that you've earned from your customers (every cookie has been good for more than three years).

You can see how profitable brand equity can be and why it's worth protecting. What's your brand equity worth? Or are you selling a generic cookie?

Random notes:

Is that with a capital "I"?

We talk and write about the Internet every day. It's a critical tool for many of us at work and home. But did you know that there are two entirely different meanings for the words *internet* and *Internet*?

The internet (with the lowercase i) is what you create any time two or more computer networks are connected. It is an inter-net, using the prefix "inter-" like you would in "international" or "interscholastic."

The Internet (with the uppercase I) is the global interconnected information system of computer networks. The World Wide Web is part of the Internet. And the Internet is the world's largest internet.

To misuse the word "internet" when you mean "Internet" or vice versa would be one of those very subtle mistakes that would speak volumes to many a critical audience. I'm sure I've made this mistake in the recent past...but not anymore!

Random notes:

I choose...

Can you envision Baskin Robbins® only carrying one flavor? Or stopping by the car dealer and discovering that all the cars are red? Hard to imagine, isn't it? According to Josh Hammond and James Morrison, authors of *The Stuff Americans Are Made Of*, Americans have treasured choice ever since the Puritans landed at Plymouth.

How do you build choice into what you offer your customers? Here are some ideas.

Features. Look at the amazing recovery Apple® enjoyed with the iMac®. Computers in a choice of colors? Computers as a design element? Absurd? Maybe, but it worked. And now look at how the PC manufacturers are scrambling to follow suit.

Access. How many different ways can your clients get in touch with you? Phone, fax, email, Web site comment form? How about your hours? Do those offer enough choice?

Price. Some customers will prefer buying from you a la carte. Others will be glad to pay a package price for a bundle of your products or services. Or some clients might opt to pay up front if they get a discount, while others will pay a premium for stretching out their payments over time.

Are you going to take my advice on this one? It's your choice!

Random notes:

An alternative to underwear

We've all heard the advice given to nervous speakers—imagine the audience in their underwear. I think there might be a less graphic way to shoo away those butterflies.

The easiest way to alleviate those pre-speech shaky knees is to be well prepared. Here are some questions to ask yourself as you write your speech.

- Why did they ask me to speak?

- How did they promote my presentation?

- How can I help the audience relate to me?

- What are they expecting? Inspiration? Facts? My personal story? Emotional support? Ideas they can use? Entertainment?

- What's the single most important piece of information that I want them to remember?

- What story or illustration can I use to cement my main point in the audience's mind?

- What do I want out of giving the speech? To be asked back? To be asked by someone in the audience to speak to their organization? Clients/contracts?

Once you know where you need to go, it will be a snap to write the speech that will get you there. Then, bye-bye butterflies!

Random notes:

First, you scratch my back

Most people look for networking opportunities so they can mine for new business. You go to a cocktail party or Chamber event, shake hands and give out business cards. Perhaps there's another way. C. Richard Weylman, author of *Endless Prospects*, touts "reverse networking." It's an interesting concept. Rather than fishing for new business, you open a fishing hole.

In a nutshell, you create opportunities for your clients or customers to meet one another and then let nature and networking takes its course. There are lots of ways to get it done.

You could host an anniversary or thank you party for all your clients so they can schmooze with one another. Or if they have common interests, you might establish an email list serve for them to share ideas. Even a simple wine and cheese event could be of tremendous value if the guests walk away with a new customer.

So often, people talk about proving marketing's value in terms of ROI. Well, with this particular idea, it will be tough. By creating extra value for your clientele, you acquire a halo of caring that increases their loyalty and boosts referrals. It may not spike the ROI chart, but it can become the conduit for them to meet prospects and new vendors. Your competitors will never be able to tempt them away from you.

Random notes:

An abbreviated state

If you're capturing names and addresses on your Web site with the intention of sending out a mailing later, pay special attention to how you create the address fields. Many Web sites, while trying to make it easy to capture each visitor's name and address use a pop-up menu that presents every state. But on many of these menus the state is spelled out. Instead of FL, it would be Florida. Instead of MN, it would be listed as Minnesota, etc.

Convenient and quick. But not good for saving money on your mailing. Automation-based discount rates are the most cost effective of the many bulk mail rates. But to qualify for that super saver rate, your mail pieces must pass CASS.

The U.S. Postal Service's CASS (Coding Accuracy Support System) checks that carrier route, 5-Digit, ZIP+4 Codes, and Delivery Point Barcodes are accurate. Everything must match up perfectly. But in order for CASS to "match" the state field, the state must be condensed to its two-character abbreviation, not spelled out.

You could have prepared everything else perfectly, but if you have the full name of the state spelled out, you're going to pay a higher mailing rate. Or have to change all your mailing labels.

So, whether you're collecting addresses on your Web site or buying a list, save yourself some time by abbreviating your states from the get-go. Or your mailing may be a no-go.

Random notes:

Try a taste

Let's face it, grocery stores are chaos on the weekends. The only ones who seem to be enjoying themselves are the sample ladies. They get to entice shoppers with bite-sized morsels of the latest offerings. The food manufacturers know that people are more likely to buy something new if they've had a chance to taste it first. Pretty smart marketing. We love to get something for free. And we love samples.

The Internet has created a whole new world of sampling. Now, with the click of a mouse, you can get free knowledge, expertise and insight.

David Allen, a productivity expert, puts this technique into practice. His ideas are insightful and easy to implement. But you don't have to take my word for it, because you can sample his ideas for yourself. Go to www.davidco.com and sign up for David's free e-newsletter.

Giving away a bit of your expertise to demonstrate your product or service makes a lot of sense. Just ask the sample ladies. And of course, ask yourself what you can offer as a sample.

Random notes:

Trading secrets

Hosting a party to show off your wares is hardly a new idea. On a small scale, it's called a Tupperware® party. On a large scale, we call it a trade show. You get away from the office, wine and dine potential clients and enjoy the added benefit of scoping out the competition. In today's tight economic times, many a CFO is questioning the expense of trade show participation. You can demonstrate the value of your trade show budget by making the most of every opportunity.

- Use the trade show host's resources. They'll be able to give you industry and demographic details about the expected attendees. You should be able to find out what trends, round table discussions and speakers will be spotlighted. How can you link your products or services to those topics?

- Get to the attendees before the show. Don't wait until they approach your booth. Reach out to the trade show attendees with a mailing that lures them to your exhibit or cocktail party.

- Keep talking. Every booth will collect business cards. Does it surprise you to know that most won't do any sort of follow-up after the show? Don't get caught in that crowd. If you think the majority of the names you've collected are not good prospects—why are you at the show?

A little extra effort before and after the trade show will have you and your CFO whistling a happy tune.

Random notes:

Come on in!

You know, in some ways the corner drugstore has a huge advantage over a service business. Every day, their customers walk right through their doors. They get to display their wares and offer additional products at the checkout counter. Service businesses, on the other hand, tend to go directly to their clients. They do it for their clients' convenience. But sometimes it's worth getting the home court advantage. If you're a service provider, why not host an open house or holiday party to welcome your clients onto your own turf. Doubtful that it's worth the effort? Remember these paybacks.

- Your guests will be surrounded by your brand.

- You can put your work on display—show off talents and service lines that your clients might not be aware of.

- Your clients will no doubt strike up conversations and since you are what they have in common, hopefully they will reinforce each other's buying decision.

- You get a chance to socialize with your clients. Something I'll bet you do not do as much of as you should.

- Perhaps most important—you can take the time to say thank you for their business.

Every once in a while, make sure you open your doors to the people who help you keep them open!

Random notes:

Paper can pack a punch

It's not uncommon to vary ink color or use a die cut to spice up a printed piece, but when was the last time you explored using a unique paper? Specialty papers are a smart choice when your budget is limited but you still want to make a splash. They can give your piece a very custom look and feel—and keep your budget numbers in line. Here are some paper terms you might bump into, as you explore specialty papers.

- **Deckle edge:** The feathered edge on paper that is produced when wet fibers are distorted on the edge of the web by a jet of water, air or suction. This is done on purpose, for aesthetic reasons and found on stationery and announcements.

- **Air-dried paper:** Paper that is dried by circulating hot air around it with little or no tension or restraint on the paper. This gives the paper a hard cockle finish typical of bond papers.

- **Felt:** A particular finish of paper, achieved by pressing a specially woven endless belt made of wool, cotton or synthetic materials against the paper during drying on a paper machine.

- **Runability:** Paper's performance on a press and its ability to withstand the stresses of a running press unaltered.

Ask your printer or your printer's paper rep to bring you sample books or invite you to the next paper fair. You'll be amazed at the options and possibilities.

Random notes:

Discover the perfect word

We all want our marketing efforts to be persuasive. We want to have impact. Sometimes it's all about choosing the right words. As Mark Twain said, "The difference between using the right word and almost the right word is like the difference between a lightning bug and lightning!"

Words, when used with skill, can create a picture as vividly as a paintbrush does.

The next time you are talking about a product or service that opens new doors or makes something possible, think about painting a picture of discovery.

The word "discovery," and the anticipation it connotes, is filled with promise. Childhood secrets and journeys yet to come. The word conveys excitement and adventure. If you tell an audience that you want to share a discovery with them, your enthusiasm becomes contagious.

Now, doesn't that sound a lot more appealing than using the expected "new and improved"?

Random notes:

Are your customers in training?

It may be that your potential customers don't buy anything from you because they don't know how to use your products or services. You can either sit around and wait for them to gain the knowledge they need, or you can take it upon yourself to train them.

Let me give you an example. Home Depot® offers free training classes practically every day of the week.

Whether it's faux painting or tiling a kitchen floor, each class walks the novice do-it-yourselfer through the project from start to finish. Now here's the smart part. Not only do they give you the skills to successfully complete your home improvement project, but they also give you a very detailed list of needed materials.

Could it get any simpler? Customers are basically given a shopping list. Guess where they shop? At least two out of every four attendees buy the products listed at Home Depot. The store reaps the sales that their classes sowed.

Look at what you sell. Could you hold classes for your potential and existing customers that would give them the confidence to buy more from you? How can you give them new knowledge and then hand them a shopping list to boot?

Random notes:

A year-end review

No matter how smart we are, how strong our team is or how big a budget we have—there's always room for improvement. Use this list of questions either as you wrap up a fiscal year or as you begin planning for the upcoming year. Go through these yourself and then identify some others in your organization who might see both the questions and the answers from a different perspective. If you're really brave, ask your clients.

- Did we articulate our brand and did we present it consistently?

- Did we always protect the integrity of our logo treatment, design and colors?

- Would someone be able to look at one of our marketing pieces and recognize it as ours because it had our consistent look, feel and tone?

- How well have we educated our current customers about our products/services? Could they list 2 or 3 that they don't currently buy from us?

- How often do we say something relevant to current clients that doesn't involve billing?

- How often, if at all, have we asked our current customers how they feel about us and our ability to meet their needs?

Don't let yourself off the hook too easily. An honest appraisal now will mean a more successful year ahead.

Random notes:

Hot sales

Sales are slow. The VP of sales is applying pressure. You and your team start brainstorming. New packaging? A national TV campaign? Coupon insert in the newspapers? Product placement in Trading Spaces®? All great ideas. But sometimes the big idea is a small one.

In his article "Quick Start Marketing Ideas," Canadian marketer Kurian M. Tharakan tells how a hot sauce producer dramatically increased sales by making one small change to its product.

They didn't change their packaging, jingle or recipe. They didn't get their product onto more store shelves. Or on Trading Spaces. They didn't get the consumer to pay more money for the product.

So, how did they increase sales? Simple. They increased the size of the holes in the top of the bottle.

Are there places or ways in your business that you could "increase the size of the holes in your bottle" to get your clients or customers to use more of your product?

Random notes:

It's got to start on the inside

Imagine an idyllic world where your customers love your products so much that they talk other people into buying it. They wear clothes bearing your logo and even plan parties to celebrate that they own something you sell. Most amazing of all—they are such rabid fans that they tattoo your logo onto their body.

I know, you're thinking I've switched to fiction. But that world exists for the Harley-Davidson Company®.

They have brilliantly manipulated and strengthened their brand and built a brand equity that most companies can only dream of having. They don't have customers, they have passionate advocates, who not only buy their motorcycles but also give them incredible amounts of free advertising (not to mention additional revenue) by owning banks, jackets, hats, lighters, travel clocks, mugs, pens, shot glasses and other items all with the Harley logo.

How did Harley-Davidson create this nirvana? By recognizing how much their brand matters and by building a corporate culture that protects and builds the equity at any cost. In other words, they earned it by making tough choices and staying the course.

Could an internal marketing department manage that coup all by itself? No. This is an all-company effort. Every Harley-Davidson employee shares the vision.

So, why am I telling you this tale? Look around. Could you stop a random employee and ask them to articulate your company's brand? How about your CEO? Is it alive and well in your break rooms? If you do nothing else—do this. Breathe life into your brand internally. Until it lives there, it can't live in the hearts of your consumers.

Well, 1,000 words is probably a slight exaggeration

An ad's picture or visual image can speak volumes. The image you choose can significantly affect readership and recall. In recall tests, it is often the visual that makes the initial impact. Keep in mind these suggestions when evaluating print ad visuals.

- Let your visual capture the mood. Visuals can be playful, romantic, wistful or even angry. Let your visual convey the emotion of your ad.

- Keep it very simple. Usually, one large image is stronger than a montage.

- Voilá. Show the before and after. Seeing is believing.

- Avoid trite images. You know the stock photography I am talking about—the one where the businessman is gesturing with his glasses.

- Add some copy. Research shows that readers go right to the captions. If you think adding a caption will deliver the message, don't shy away.

Think of the headline and visual as the lures. If they can hook the audience, the copy can close the deal. But without that hook, the copy doesn't get a chance and you don't get the sale.

Random notes:

Come on back y'all!

Customers come and go. Depending on the kind of business you're in, your customer cycle might be only a few days or a year or more. But you shouldn't lose track of those former customers. Even if they left because they were unhappy for some reason.

If you're routinely purging past customers from your database, you're tossing away an incredibly cost-effective source of revenue and business insight. You might be able to win some of them back...and you can pick their brains on how to make your business even better.

Why not try a lost-customer survey?

The lost-customer survey asks open-ended questions to probe reasons for dissatisfaction. According to Terry Vavra in the book *Aftermarketing*, response rates to such a survey often reach 35 to 50%. People want to share their opinion and they feel valued for being asked. Vavra advises you to resist the temptation to ask directly, "How can we win you back?"

Carefully study the results of your survey. I'll be stunned if the insights you gain don't alter the way you do business in some way.

A second mailing after the survey can report findings that prompted some changes. After you've demonstrated how well you listened, you can ask for another chance. This is a win-win situation. Your business gets better and you'll probably win back a customer or two.

Random notes:

What did you say, Sonny?

People 50+ spend more than $1 trillion a year on products and services, and that number will only get larger. For the next 18 years, one baby boomer will turn 50 every 7.5 seconds. Now that's a significant group of consumers. Want to know how to win their favor?

- Remember their physical challenges. Anything you print should be designed with their 50+ eyes in mind. Increase the type size on labels, use contrasting colors, and stay away from fancy fonts and clutter.

- No funny business. They'll call you on hype and hyperbole in a heartbeat. Just be straightforward and don't insult their intelligence. Avoid sounding condescending.

- Don't assume they are all the same. A 50-year-old is markedly different from a 75-year-old. You'll have to do quite a bit of sub-segmenting to address their varying wants and needs. And don't talk to them only in terms of their age. Remember all the usual breakdowns like income, ethnicity, health, discretionary time, etc.

This audience can yield some big revenue for smart marketers. Just remember, these people are not addle-brained or out of touch. They're used to being catered to and will demand the respect they deserve. Be sure to give it to them.

Random notes:

Hold them at the edge of their seat

Is it just me, or have business presentations gotten a lot worse lately? I think because we now have all kinds of high-tech solutions, business execs have gotten lazy. Sure, Power Point is a fine tool. But it hardly takes the place of a well-crafted speech.

The key to a presentation that will hold attention is doing your homework and prepping. Try some of these low-tech solutions.

- Weave a story. A heartwarming or compelling tale is the best way to illustrate a point. If you're using charts, graphs and columns of numbers, don't stop there. Behind those statistics is a story. Dig it up and tell it.

- Keep the audience alert. If you are going to use a projector or slides, be mindful of how dark the room is and raise the lights as soon as you can.

- Narrow your focus to no more than four key points. Mention these points at the beginning, use them as anchor points in the middle and sum them up at the end.

- Don't let the audience cheat. If they have your handouts before you're done, you're done. Your presentation shouldn't need a cheat sheet. Give them the handouts as you're walking out.

Leave the audience with something to remember you by. End with a bang. Challenge them. Chastise them. Inspire them. But don't leave on a dull note.

Random notes:

Secrets of the elusive male shopper

We've all observed it. We probably even joked about it. While the stereotype that all men hate to shop is an exaggeration, there is truth to the suggestion that many men are uncomfortable shopping and their behavior proves it. *Why We Buy: The Science of Shopping* by Paco Underhill suggests a wise storekeeper can use that discomfort to their advantage.

- A man hates to ask for the department or item he wants in a store. He'd rather leave if he can't find it on his own.

So does this factoid scream good signage to you? Directional signs will keep that male customer from walking out, frustrated because he couldn't find what he was looking for. In addition, your store (or online store) should be laid out so shoppers can intuitively find what they're looking for.

- If a man tries something on, he'll buy it 65% of the time.

If a guy goes to all the trouble of actually trying something on, he wants it to be easy. Having enough dressing rooms is key. Another hint. Don't lock them. If your male shopper has to find a clerk with a key, odds are he's going to bail on you.

- Only 25% of men will grocery shop with a list.

This means a couple different things. One—men are habitual impulse buyers. Keep your end-of-aisle displays full. Second, it means they are at risk of forgetting things. You'll become a lifesaver and men's store of choice if you jog their memory with little signs by the ground beef that say, "Don't forget the buns" or "Need ketchup?"

Men may not like to shop, but once they find a store that makes it comfortable and convenient, they're a very loyal bunch.

Random notes:

Let your fingers do the walking

Many of you are probably too young to recognize the above reference to an old Yellow Pages® slogan. But the message still rings true. When you are proofing anything that includes a phone number, take the extra minute and actually dial the number to check its accuracy.

Mail order giant L.L. Bean® drills home the importance of proofreading to all its employees. So far, so good. But, an overzealous employee almost caused a disaster because he skipped the "dial it first" step. He was 100% positive that a toll-free number starting with 877 should really start with 800, so he changed it.

Somehow that employee hadn't heard that toll-free numbers could now begin with 877 as well as 800 or 888. Had he not mentioned it to another employee right before they went to press, hundreds of thousands of catalogs would have been printed wrong.

Are you having more than one person proof any communications tool you're creating? Assuming that's true, implement this policy. The first proofreader dials the number to make sure it's correct, then initials it. That signals to the other proofreaders that the number has been verified.

A misprint of a wrong phone number is 100% avoidable. Don't let yourself get that sloppy.

Random notes:

What do they say about lemonade?

That beautiful four-color brochure just came back from the printer. You are showing it off like a proud papa. Until someone points out the typo.

Now what? If you have a huge budget and aren't against a deadline, you can reprint. But that's probably unrealistic for most of us. So, you have to find a way to make it work.

Many people will suggest solutions that try to "hide" the mistake. You know, put a sticker over the erroneous type with the correct type. Yuck. All that does is scream, "Hey look at our mistake! We think you're dumb enough not to notice!"

Consider creating a sticker or insert that announces, "Can you find the typo?" Sure, it's exposing your mistake to everyone, but it also has the advantage of getting your audience to read each word very carefully.

Make it a contest. Include an email address, fax number or URL so readers can contact you with the correct answer. Then do a drawing among all those who got it right.

Is it ideal? Nope. But, it beats having people thinking you didn't see it. Work it to your advantage and make the prize they win a sample of something you've been trying to sell them all along.

Random notes:

It's all about me

Too many brand managers think that their product or service's brand is actually about the product or service. They're confusing product attributes with brand association. Tiffany & Co.® has an open-heart pendant that is 18K gold on a 16" silk cord. That's the product. The fact that they can charge $875 for that necklace is all about their brand.

A brand is a relationship. It's not just an attribute in a vacuum. It's about how I interact with the brand and what that says about me, the consumer. I could buy an open-heart necklace on a silk cord from many places. But, what does buying that necklace at Tiffany's say about me? Or what does it say to the person I buy it for? That's the power of the brand.

This isn't just about luxury products or companies. Want some more examples? What adjectives would you use to describe someone who buys jewelry at K-Mart®? Or a person who uses a Mac® computer? How about someone who shops on QVC®? Eats Ben & Jerry's® ice cream?

And this isn't just true for products. How would you describe an H&R Block® tax customer? Or someone who gets their car's oil changed at a Grease Monkey®? What do you know about a Hotwire.com℠ client?

Imagine the importance of knowing what your brand says about your consumers. If it's on target, you can enhance it. If it's off base or keeps people from buying—then you need to fix it.

Just remember as you explore this topic, look for adjectives that describe your consumers, not your products or services. It's all about them.

Random notes:

Give me a boost!

Remember when you were a kid and you'd give your friends a boost by lacing your fingers together and letting them step into your cupped hands? They could reach new heights. Sometimes a company's branding efforts need a helping hand to keep them moving forward as well.

This is where a classic tagline or theme can boost your ongoing branding efforts. Most companies wimp out when it comes to a tagline. They choose something that could just as easily be said by their competitors or even a business in another category. The discipline of identifying a few key words that communicate the full weight and force of your brand message is one of the cornerstones to creating a successful brand.

Take a look at your current tagline. How well does it stand up to these three tough questions?

- Does it provide a clear, recognizable and sustainable differentiation from the competition?

- Does it respond to your customers' most pressing needs in a compelling, believable manner?

- Does it provide guidance for your company's management decision-making, hiring, training and resource allocation?

Random notes:

We're simple creatures

We humans have a tendency to make the simple appear complicated. But, when you boil it all down, all human decisions are motivated by one of eight considerations:

- Time/convenience
- Money
- Recovering something lost (like youth)
- Sex
- Knowledge/self-improvement
- Security/safety
- Comfort
- Care of loved ones

The real trick is not memorizing this list but understanding how your product or service satisfies one of these core needs.

Once you have that answer, you probably have the essential message for your marketing efforts, eh?

Commerce is out, culture is in

Too many business people dismiss the Internet because they run a local business or sell a product or service that can't be sold online. That's ridiculous. I think the hype and predictions that everyone was going to buy everything online has passed. People now understand it's not about where people buy. It's about where people communicate.

Business leaders need to stop thinking about e-commerce and begin to understand e-culture. The Internet is changing everything, including the way people think, communicate and interact. They log on to get information and share experiences. Many surfers have found online communities that fill their needs, both personal and professional.

If you haven't used an IM product or read a blog, you'd better catch up. They're not just for teenagers or geeks anymore. AOL® adds more than 10,000 new users a day. MSN® now has more than 10 million members. And that's only two providers.

How are you keeping current on e-culture? Do you know how it has already changed your business? How it has changed your consumers? Can you anticipate how it will change the future? If you don't, your competition will.

Random notes:

Nothing remote
about the advantages

Radio remotes, where radio station personalities broadcast live from your business location, have been around for a long time. And their popularity is growing. Radio has an interesting juxtaposition inherent to it. There's an intimacy that listeners feel toward the radio DJ they listen to every day. The on-air personalities talk about their lives, families and even their vacations. So naturally listeners feel like they really know the DJ.

On the other hand, because it is an audio-only medium, the listener rarely gets to actually see their friend, the on-air talent. That creates incredible curiosity. So, when there is a remote, and the on-air talent is saying, "Come on down to Big Bob's...we'll be here until 1 p.m. today giving away tickets and CDs"—the draw is almost undeniable. And so they come.

A remote can be a very wise marketing move. Typically for a flat fee, you get a 2 to 3 hour remote with 1 or 2 on-air personalities at your location, and you'll be interviewed at least a couple of times during the remote. During each live break back to the remote location, the announcer will talk about you and your business. You'll also get a bank of radio spots and plenty of station promotional plugs throughout the week prior to the remote. That's a lot of editorial value wrapped up in an advertising package.

Don't forget about this option. Remotes are perfect for grand openings, annual sales or just when you want to create a lot of buzz and traffic at your location.

Random notes:

You ought to be in pictures

Never before have marketers had so many different ways to communicate their message. Each option comes with its unique advantages and downsides. One that is often overlooked or erroneously dismissed as being too expensive or perhaps not high-tech enough is the production of a video. In reality, the return on the investment can be significant.

A well-produced video can deliver the following benefits:

- Delivers the intimacy of extended one-to-one communication.

- Is not interrupted by advertising or station breaks.

- Can be used to do long-distance training.

- Communicates a consistent message to an audience separated by time or distance.

- Allows three-dimensional views of products.

- Demonstrates a product in use or a service provider in action.

- Captures and conveys emotion with the powerful combination of visual and audio cues.

- Can be combined with CD, DVD or streaming video technology to translate to an easy direct mail piece or Web page content.

Videos are an extremely powerful way to communicate with your employees, board of directors, clients or potential clients. Don't disregard this marketing workhorse.

Random notes:

Be a do-gooder

Companies, big and small, tend to be generous. They might sponsor a little league team or donate their products and services to a community struck by flooding. For many years, community giving and marketing seemed to be tied together by a dotted line. But not any more.

Many savvy businesses are now using their charitable giving as a marketing tool. And with good reason. For some, the dollars they donate to various charities would add up to a sizeable advertising budget. There's nothing wrong with benefiting from the associated goodwill of that generosity.

Cause marketing is all about building your image and your bottom-line through socially responsible partnerships, programs and events. It doesn't work if it's not sincere or something the whole company is invested in.

If you are looking for a charity that's the right fit for your organization, there's a Web site that can help— www.networkforgood.com. It has a search engine that will allow you to use key words, charitable categories and geographical perimeters to find charities that are a good match. If you happen to be a nonprofit, you might check to make sure you are listed.

Giving feels good. It can also be good for business.

No comment

When a company official says "no comment," 58% of the public believes the company is guilty of the accusation. That is a damning statement about our culture and the power of the media today.

Robin Cohn's book, *The PR Crisis Bible* tells a story that really drives home this message. One day a CEO heard someone behind him say, "Excuse me." Turning around, he recognized a well-known business reporter who said, "I just have one question."

The CEO panicked, said "no comment" and rushed away from the reporter.

With all the scandals of the day, the phrase "no comment" now implies a cover up. The reporter, who was only going to ask for directions to an employee's office, got suspicious and started making some phone calls. He found a disgruntled employee and looked for dirt on the Internet. He ended up writing an exposé of problems at the company and the stock price dropped like a rock.

What should you say instead of no comment? Try "We'll have a statement for you later when we have all the facts," or something to that effect.

Random notes:

Why is it so hard to do nothing?

One of the marketing gospels that I will preach until the end of time is not to pull the plug too soon. Stay the course. For some reason, this is a particularly difficult thing for people to do. There is an inherent impatience that trips up good marketing efforts every day. You run an ad a couple of times and then if you don't get a response—you pull it. You leave a couple of messages on someone's voice mail and if they don't get back to you, you cross them off the list.

Remember…you get tired of your message much quicker than your audience does. Heck, by the time you're tired of it, they are noticing it for the first time! There is research that suggests an ad has to run on average, 8-13 times before there is any audience recall at all.

Even after they've noticed the ad or Web banner or direct mail piece, people might not need you right now. But what would happen if you stopped talking to them at that point? By the time they do need you, they've forgotten all about you!

If you really want someone's business, you need to consistently stay in touch. That way, when the person is ready to do business, your company will be at the top of his or her mind. From there, you still have to earn the business, but at least the consistent message got you the necessary attention.

Tell your story. And then tell it again. And again.

Random notes:

It just doesn't work

You've all battled it. Someone in HR wants to turn your logo yellow because it will look better on the blue shirt. The typeface that you use for your company name? The guys in IT want to change it to something more trendy and Web friendly. Or the new CEO hates brown, especially the shade of your corporate color. Guess what's high on his priority list?

Next time people want you to change your corporate identity, try this. Buy a can of Coke® and place it on their office desk. Give them 30 seconds to study it and then tell them to close their eyes and picture the Coke can in their minds. Then wait a few seconds and ask them to imagine the can of Coke looking exactly the same, except it's green.

They'll tell you it's just wrong. The can has to be red or it isn't Coke.

There's your ah-ha moment. Tell them they can open their eyes and when they do, simply smile at them and say, "And that's why we don't change the color of our logo either."

Companies invest a significant amount of money and effort into creating a brand. A big part of brand awareness and recognition is the visual cues, like color or typeface. If companies like McDonalds® and Coke don't mess with theirs, why in the world would you?

Next time you or a coworker thinks about messing with your visual identity, go buy yourself a can of Coke and set it on your desk. Then, just leave everything be.

Random notes:

It sounds just like you

Oftentimes, how you say something is more important than what you say.

For most companies, it is much easier for them to identify and describe their visual identity than it is their company's voice. Every company, large or small, has a natural tenor. It is an extension of your company's brand. It's the embodiment of your company's soul. Are you authoritative? Compassionate? Paternal? Affable? Conspiratorial?

If you were any one of those, would you use formal language or be conversational? Would you use short, choppy sentences or long, descriptive paragraphs? Would you adhere to grammar and style rules or take some liberties? Would you use slang or industry jargon?

Regardless of how many different writers are involved, your materials should always be in the same voice. Have you ever read an ad or brochure and then said, "Boy, that just doesn't sound like them"? That's because the writer couldn't capture the company's tone. Most likely, the company hadn't done the homework of identifying and articulating what their voice was.

No matter how you find it, it's imperative that you dig deep enough to find your company's natural voice. Your customers and employees may not be able to describe what you should sound like, but boy, will they notice when you get it wrong.

Random notes:

It isn't just for ads anymore!

You thought I was done harping on that voice stuff, didn't you? Well, almost.

Too many people think that as long as their ads, brochures or Web sites are written in their true voice, they're covered. Wrong.

This isn't an advertising or marketing voice. It's the embodiment of what your company's all about. It should be consistent everywhere. Internal, External. Anytime your company communicates, it should be authentic.

Have you checked the voice of these communications tools?

- How your company phone is answered
- Employee manual
- Signage
- Signature line on company emails
- Press releases
- On hold message
- Annual report
- Fax cover sheet

Now that I've got your motor running, what other elements of your company should also be voice checked?

Random notes:

Your computer is infected, click here now

Banner and pop-up ads. They can be annoying, but they can also be effective. One of the great questions still plaguing marketing professionals is how do you harness the power and potential of the Internet? One of the most widely used—and misused—methods is the banner or pop-up ad.

Banner ads are a lot like traditional direct mail. Response rates can vary from 1 to 2% (which is considered acceptable) to more than 30%.

Here are six tips for creating a banner or pop-up ad that works:

- Keep it simple.

- Animate for good reason, not just because you can.

- Use bright and unusual colors.

- Surprise is the best element. Use humor or facts to get their attention.

- Make it interactive, if it's appropriate.

- Have a strong call to action.

Another thing you'll want to do is change your creative design frequently. Yahoo® studies report declining effectiveness after only two weeks.

Random notes:

Don't get in your own way

When you're writing copy, be it for an ad, brochure, Web site or direct mail piece, it's important to identify, before the first keystroke, what you want the recipient to know.

Make a list of the three most important things you want someone to remember after they've been exposed to your message. No, you can't cheat and have four. After you have the top three, rank them according to importance. Then cross off #3.

We humans have incredibly short attention spans and our brains are overflowing with information. So there's not a lot of extra room. At best, most people are going to remember one or two things.

Does this mean you should only have a headline and a couple bullet points? No. It means make sure, either in how you write the copy (perhaps repetition) or in the layout of the piece, that your two main points are front and center.

If you want them to take action or remember a benefit—don't muddy up your message by hiding it among many messages. Be clear about the result you want. And then, don't get in its way.

Random notes:

It's not called wasted space... it's called white space

Every day, in every newspaper across the land, there is an ad that is so crammed with copy that your eyes practically cross when you look at it.

If you are guilty of creating an ad like that—shame on you. I don't care who insisted that the additional paragraph get shoved in there, it's still wrong. And a waste of money because no one is going to respond to that ad.

You know the ads I'm talking about. If someone were asked to describe them, they'd use words like full, cramped, crammed, packed or stuffed. Do you really want any of those words associated with your product or service? It looks like you were too cheap to buy the proper-sized ad.

A print ad absolutely must be appealing to the eye. No, that doesn't mean it has to be pretty. It just means there should be some balance between the type and the white space around it. If you have to reduce the font or condense the leading of your type to fit all the copy in, you are creating an ad that the eye will naturally avoid.

The test for this one is easy. Let your eyes glance over the ad. They'll either be naturally drawn to start reading the copy or they'll bounce around a little, not sure where to go next because there's no break in the blur of type.

If that's the case, call your ad rep. It's time to buy a bigger ad!

Random notes:

It's $19.99. Want to buy it?

Sooner or later, you have to tell the customers how much your product or service is going to cost. And you know it's a reasonable price. Or maybe it's a real bargain. But do they know it yet?

No matter what you're selling, a price has no meaning until your audience knows what they're getting and why they should buy it. Unless you are so well known that you're practically a commodity, don't lead with your price. First, talk about the problem you are going to solve or the basic need you are going to meet. Demonstrate your product's benefits and give the potential buyer a chance to want it before you try to sell it.

Then, without any embarrassment or hesitation, tell them the cost. Proudly. Because you know it's a good price and you've now exhibited the value you're going to deliver.

Want a lesson in superb copywriting about price? Read a Land's End® catalog. The headline over a pair of shoes said, "Introducing new hand-sewn Mocs. Quality craftsmanship, value-priced." And if that didn't convince you to buy the shoes, they ended their little blurb with, "The price? A refreshingly honest $29.50." Before they tell you the price, they spend 60 words reassuring you of the shoes' quality.

They're so darned proud of their prices that you can't help but feel like you are getting a bargain. That's nimble marketing.

Random notes:

Riddle me this

People are very curious about themselves and each other. Which is why the media loves surveys.

You can create a significant amount of buzz for your company by releasing some research data. Your research does not need to be some massive, scientifically rigorous tome to generate media attention. There is definitely a proper time and place for quality market research. But, in this case, I'm talking about just polling your customers with an interesting question that does not have an obvious answer so you can get some press coverage.

How might this work for you? Try these on for size.

- Real estate agent: What one item turns a house into a home for you?

- Corporate trainer: If you could make one training course mandatory for your entire company, what topic would you choose?

- Electronics Store: What one piece of electronic equipment could you not do without?

- Accountant: How confident are you that you saved as much money as you legally could on your taxes last year?

You can see how a reporter looking for a filler story might easily pick up the results of this sort of poll. It is also interesting enough that you could create a mailing for your clients or prospects. Demonstrate how you can fill the need expressed by the poll answers.

If nothing else, it's an excellent conversation starter to get to know your clients better.

Random notes:

Exposed on all sides

For most businesses, you haven't had to worry about international communications all that often. But the Internet is changing things. Your Web site can be viewed anywhere in the world, even by those visitors whose computer is not configured for English.

Which means their browser may or may not recognize all the characters and symbols as you originally typed them. This is particularly vexing when it comes to characters like the copyright symbol.

While most browsers on the Internet can display the © symbol, it is probably safest to include both the symbol and the written copyright notice on your site.

Random notes:

Traffic jam wanted?

You labored over it. It's full of useful information. It even has some cool graphics. Now all you need are the surfers. First, we need to understand why people are online in the first place. According to a recent study, 77% of people surfing the Web are looking for information.

How do you use that fact to drive traffic to your site? Think about the ways potential and on-going customers seek you out when they need information. Make sure your URL is present in all those instances.

- Answering machine or voice mail messages
- Your email signature
- Outdoor signage at your physical location
- Your sign-off when you participate in topic-related list serves
- Fax cover sheet
- Annual reports
- Letterhead, business cards, report covers
- Presentation slides
- Yellow Page ads
- Shopping bags
- Bill inserts
- Invoices

Once you get your audience to your site, make sure they want to stay. Load it with useful documents that can be downloaded. Let them interact by participating in discussions or a poll. Give away samples of your product or service. Make it easy for them to email you with questions.

In other words, give them the information they're looking for and they'll keep coming back for more.

Random notes:

Flattery will get you everywhere

No one likes to be called lazy, stupid or some other unattractive trait. But, compliment their acute sense of style or the deft way they handle difficult situations and you've got them eating out of your hand. People like to think of themselves as being well above average. A smart copywriter can play to that vanity to capture someone's attention.

I was recently skimming a newsletter (*The Manager's Intelligence Report*) and had to laugh and appreciate the newsletter editor's insight into this notion of taking advantage of their readers' self-image.

Like most newsletters these days, it has a very *USA Today* feel. Short articles and lots of graphics. I tend to skim it, catching headlines and bits of copy. But, the center spread had a large, bold subtitle that immediately caught my eye...and had me reading the entire section word for word.

The subtitle—"For Achievers Only." Now, what manager is going to skip over that section? I sure knew there was going to be something in that article that pertained to me! After all, I'm an achiever, right?

How could you use this quirk of human nature to get your prospect's attention?

Random notes:

It may be free,
but it isn't cheap!

Think about the advice you've given your customers over the years. You've probably answered hundreds of questions on topics related to your business. No doubt, your customers have valued that information.

It might be even more valuable than you realize.

Take ten minutes to brainstorm the most common questions you've been asked about the products or services that your company sells. Then, jot down the answers. Now, poll your coworkers who have the most contact with your clients. See what questions and answers they can add to the list. Once you've compiled all the data, see if there's a logical way to arrange the questions and do so.

Once you have the information written and formatted in a way that makes sense to you, show it to someone outside your company to make sure your answers are very clear and helpful.

Voila! You've just created a question-and-answer tip sheet or, in Internet lingo, an FAQ (frequently asked questions) sheet.

Now, print your FAQ sheet and mail it to your database of current customers. Or post it on your Web site. Or use it as a new business mailing. Or leave some at your reception desk. Or include them with your next round of invoices. Offer it to a reporter as a possible story.

You get the idea—find a way to show your customers and potential customers the depth of your company's expertise.

Random notes:

Brochures blues?

They are one of the great workhorses of marketing. Seems like practically everyone has one, no matter what you sell. Most of them are like generic vanilla ice cream. It beats a rice cake by a long shot but it's nothing you'd rush out to buy again. If you could superimpose someone else's logo over yours and the brochure would still make sense, you're not alone. But, that's a lot of money to invest in printing just to have a generic brochure.

Want to put some pizzazz into your collateral piece? Try these:

- There is no reason to put the entire story on the cover. Keep it concise. And please, avoid clichés like "committed to customer satisfaction" or "your satisfaction is our business." Blech.

- Remember, one of the advantages of a brochure is that you have more room. Use the brochure's natural spread. If you have a barrel fold, you could have one long graphic element that spans the entire piece. Don't be afraid to cross that seam.

- Break up the copy with subheads. Think of them as the outline for your piece. Could someone only read the subheads and still get the main point? If so, you know almost everyone who picks up your brochure will get the message.

- Use design elements, like shaded boxes or shapes, to add visual power. Don't be afraid to experiment. How about a brochure that emulates a magazine layout? That would be refreshing and unique.

Once you've finished writing and designing the piece, pick it up as though you've never seen it before. Read it through and then ask yourself, "What do they want me to do?" If you can't answer that question, make sure you go back and add a very blatant call to action.

Random notes:

What did that Shakespeare guy say about roses?

I've been involved in several projects that included creating the name of a business. I can't think of a marketing decision that is more subjective or personal. That just makes it even tougher. If you ever find yourself involved in naming a business, don't forget these basics.

- Unless you choose something offensive, it's highly unlikely that anyone will do business with you because of your name. Same goes for not doing business with you.

- Flip through the phone book some time and you will be astonished at how many people thought it was a brilliant plan to choose a name that started with AAA or A+ or some variation of that theme. Do yourself a favor and just pick a name you like and create a yellow pages ad that will get you noticed. Even if your company name is Zithers R Us.

- Make it easy to say and easy to remember. Have you noticed how we tend to shorten company names? What law firm actually gets called Withers, Jones, Pratt, Smathers and Gould, except by the person who answers their phone? To everyone else, it becomes the Withers law firm. Think about how your consumers might shorten your name. Make sure you like the sound of that too.

- Unless you have a whole lot of money to spend on advertising, do not make up a word like Xerox®. You don't want to spend all your marketing dollars explaining what your name means.

Your name is just the beginning. It's an important decision but not an all consuming one. No matter what name you select, make sure you protect it legally. Or you might have to go through the whole process all over again!

Random notes:

Is .com that big of a deal?

In a word, yes. Sure, there's .net, .cc, .biz and an ever-growing host of others. But when you think of a Web address, what's the suffix you naturally assume? Right—.com. When you see a Web address with a .biz or .cc ending, what do you think? Start up? How legit are they? There's something just not quite as legitimate about it. If you saw a URL that was www.ford.cc wouldn't you assume that it just couldn't be associated with Ford Motor Company?

In many ways, it's the same with toll free numbers. I'm sorry but 877 does not create the same perception as 800. An 888 prefix is close, sort of like .net is for Web addresses. But neither one quite makes it as an equal substitute. In reality, they serve the exact same function. But that's not all that important. It's about the consumer's perception.

So what do you do if the Web address you want is already taken? First, explore if it is being used. If not, you can probably negotiate a purchase. If it is being used, do some brainstorming. Could you use hyphens? Could you add another descriptive word, like your state, to make the distinction?

If at all possible, secure a URL that ends in .com or, if you must, .net. The perception is worth the effort.

Random notes:

Why not just leave the left side blank?

For as long as people have been buying newspaper or magazine ads, there has been an assumed truth that print ads located on the left-hand page of the spread will not get read or score as well on a recall test as an ad on the right side. In fact, some publications will charge you a premium placement fee for right-sided pages. Great added revenue source for them, nonsense for you and me.

A recent study shows that there is less than a 2.1% difference in average reader interest for left versus right pages.

The study went on to say that the #1 factor in influencing readership is creativity. I know that isn't a startling revelation. The litmus test is what it's always been. Does your ad catch the reader's eye? Does the headline lure the person in? Is your visual arresting? That's what affects readership. And over time, sales.

From now on, rather than sweating page placement, put your sweat where it actually matters. Into the creation of an ad the readers can't help but notice.

Cooperation not competition?

It hardly seems like business if there's not a dog eating a dog somewhere. The recent economic climate has caused many businesses to close ranks and turn their backs on anyone who won't hand them a buck. I can't help but think that will come back to haunt them.

Business partnerships are contagious. If you help someone else be successful, it will always come back to you. Synergy. Win/Win. All recent marketing buzzwords. But the truth is, it's always been more fun when you work collaboratively.

Not only is it more fun, but it can be very successful. Partnerships are an inexpensive and effective way to leverage your own marketability as well as someone else's. Of course, they're doing the same thing with your high profile—so everyone gains new ground.

It doesn't have to be a joint business venture where everyone takes a big risk. Maybe it's as simple as the local bank serving cookies and coffee from the bakery around the corner, and, in return, the bakery hanging the bank's special CD rate poster in its window. Or maybe it's much more elaborate. That's up to you.

I think the reason most people don't partner more is simply because they don't think to. Look around at your business associates, vendors and clients. Who could you team up with?

What could you do together that neither of you could do alone? Isn't that a pretty interesting question, especially in tough economic times?

Random notes:

Ladies, start your carts!

In our American culture, it's a stereotype that women are good shoppers, but that stereotype is borne out in Paco Underhill's book *Why We Buy: The Science of Shopping.* The author made some fascinating observations that will have you seeing your business a little differently.

- For women, shopping is communal. They like to shop in pairs or in a pack. Statistically, they'll buy more when they are with someone else who's there to encourage the purchases. However, groups of 3 or more tend to be browsers, because they aren't all going to want to look at the same things for any length of time.

- Unlike men, women want to interact with the store personnel. They want information and personal service. Buyers stay in the store longer than lookers, so keep them engaged and in the store. You should have twice as many sales people in a women's clothing section as you do in the men's department.

- Women gravitate to stores that provide seating for reluctant significant others or have a department (like electronics) that will keep their mates occupied so they won't feel rushed.

- If women cannot touch it, they are not likely to buy it.

Make one change based on the four insights above and watch what happens. For those of you with an e-store, how could you apply these ideas on your Web site?

Random notes:

Liar, liar pants on fire

When a particularly outrageous commercial comes on, my daughter will roll her eyes at the TV and declare that they're lying. And she's only 10. We are a skeptical and jaded audience. Most of us have grown up with media hype and have learned to disregard much of it.

Many marketing pros forget this. They wonder if readers/viewers can tell when they are stretching the truth a little. And, they rationalize, if they put their ads in a reputable publication—they can "buy" a little credibility.

Wrong.

In a recent study, it was discovered that only 41% of readers believe most of what they read in the *Wall Street Journal*. And it scored the best of all the publications named! *Time* magazine only scored 29%, and *Newsweek* earned a 24% believability rating.

So what do you do about that? Don't hype promises or outlandish claims. Be mindful of superlatives and tired clichés. Instead, be authentic. Know your company's voice and style and be ready to deliver what you promise.

How crazy is it really?

Sometimes you have to do something a bit crazy to get your consumer's attention.

Phil Romano, the owner of an Italian restaurant, is living proof of this fact. Thanks to a little savvy insanity, his place is always packed on Mondays and Tuesdays, which is typically a dead night for restaurants.

How'd he do it? On a randomly chosen Monday or Tuesday, his dining customers received a letter instead of a bill. The letter stated that because the restaurant's mission was to make people feel like guests—it didn't seem right to always charge them for their food. Every month, on a random Monday or Tuesday, this happened. How long do you think it took before everyone in town knew?

For the relatively low cost of one night's worth of free dinners, Romano had a full house eight nights a month when all the other restaurants in town were empty. And he didn't have to spend a dime on advertising.

All of a sudden crazy sounds pretty smart, doesn't it?

Random notes:

A blank slate

You know the feeling. You've got a deadline looming. Suddenly it seems like there are 326 pieces of paper on your desk that require your immediate attention, and that email chain letter is calling your name. Writer's block. When the key you hit most often is the backspace, you know you need something to shake things loose.

We've all been there. Here are some of my favorite blockbusters.

- Just start writing and don't go back and edit. This is much harder than it sounds. But do that for at least five minutes. Go through your rough copy, circle what you like and keep going. It's much easier to rewrite than it is to start from scratch.

- Talk it through. Explain what you are trying to communicate to a coworker. Your conversation will help you get to the main points you need to cover.

- Get away from your desk for 10 minutes. Grab a snack, take a quick walk, call a friend. Or do a menial task, like filing. Sometimes when you turn off your brain, it auto starts on its own.

When you write for a living, you don't have the luxury of waiting for the muses to strike. Find a blockbuster that works for you and get back to it!

Random notes:

The eyes have it

Web design has evolved many times. And while a cool Web site is great, having an effective site is even better. So, how do people actually view Web sites?

Using a combination of complex hardware and data analysis, eye-tracking tests map a person's eye movements across a computer screen and assess the amount of mental strain exerted moment by moment. It does this by recording scanning patterns of the eye, measuring pupil dilation (which correlates to cognitive effort) and taking more than 250 observations of each eye per second.

Here's what the eye-tracking tests revealed:

- Web visitors look to the upper middle of the home page first. Over 20% of their attention is focused here. Putting your navigation tools or key content here makes sense.

- Most surfers have developed an eye pattern sequence. They look at the upper center of the page, to the left of center and then to the right of center. You could sort your information into these areas by their relative importance.

- When asked to find a specific piece of information, users' eyes stayed on the Web page for approximately 11 seconds before moving on. This means you'd better make navigation and your content incredibly easy to find.

These tests remind us that, not unlike traditional print pieces, our Web site should be intuitively geared to make it easy for our audience to find what it's looking for. Or else we'll lose their attention. All in the blink of an eye.

Random notes:

P.S. Do I have your attention now?

Many businesses use a pitch or sales letter. It's a cost effective way to get your message directly to the people or businesses that you think are the most likely targets for your product or service. But those folks get compelling letters every day. How do you get an edge that makes yours more effective?

Add a postscript.

Research has shown that a postscript is one of the first (and sometimes only) elements that the reader looks at. So, use that P.S. to restate your offer, add a bonus to your offer, or drive home a deadline. Just make sure that you don't turn it into another paragraph or disclaimer. It's prime real estate, so don't waste it!

If your P.S. is intriguing enough—it might pique the skimming reader's interest and draw him or her back up into the body of your letter. You can add color or increase the font size or style to draw additional attention to your postscript as well.

P.S. Would it be too much to actually remind you how critical the postscript is in a postscript? You're probably right.

Random notes:

It ain't over 'til it's over!

And sometimes, it's just not over. When a new media emerges, people begin predicting the demise of the traditional media of the day. When television first arrived, everyone assumed that radio was done. While radio is not the same as it was, it is still thriving today.

As the Internet emerged as a force, the Chicken Littles of the world predicted the end of newspapers. Why would anyone want generic content when they could customize their own news, 24 hours a day? Well, apparently there's some life in the old girl yet.

A recent study shows that about 80% of adults read a newspaper on a daily basis. Readership in younger age demographics is down, but that's not a new trend.

When you are planning a mass media campaign, don't rule out newspaper. You can do a lot more than just an ROP (run of press) ad, like making use of special sections, inserts and wraps. You have lots of options. And remember, it's not just the dailies. There are more niche publications out there than ever before. Whether you want business to business or lifestyle papers—they are out there and they are being read.

If you want the best of both worlds, why not place an ad in the newspaper and on its online version. The combination of the two will be pretty potent.

Random notes:

The envelope please

Believe it or not...there are entire books written about the variety of envelopes and different uses for the variations. As I flipped through one, I came upon a huge glossary of envelope jargon. A good many terms were new to me. See how many of these you know.

- **B.R.E. (I started with an easy one):** Business Reply Envelope. This usually has a first-class permit, indicia and return address preprinted on envelope. Most often it is a #9- or #10-sized envelope. A #10 is what people typically refer to as a legal-sized envelope and a #9 is the envelope that fits perfectly into a #10.

- **Converting:** The process of producing a custom-sized or specially designed envelope or any type of envelope not available in a manufacturer's standard line.

- **Flush cut:** To cut the top flap off the envelope.

- **Counted down:** To box envelopes with flaps down, as opposed to flaps extended.

- **Blank:** Paper stock that is die cut into appropriate envelope shape. When folded and glued, it becomes an envelope.

- **M weight:** The weight of one thousand pieces—either a specific type of envelope or sheet of a grade of paper in its basic size.

- **Thumb cut:** A notched opening to allow easy access to contents.

This is one of those "you'll never know you need to know it until you need to know it" categories. Or, who knows, it might save you in a close Trivial Pursuit® game!

Random notes:

yourbusiness.com? Maybe

More than 2 billion Web sites communicate every day. Shouldn't your business be one of them?

There's been a lot of noise made about how no one, save the porn sites, is making any money on the Web. Whether or not you can make money is just one of the questions you should ask yourself as you consider the possibility of creating a Web presence. Make sure you ask yourself these questions as well:

- What are the costs to you if you don't have a Web site?

- Could you provide a service to your current customers over the Web?

- What other key audiences could you communicate with?

- Are you ready to devote the resources to maintain a site?

The benefits are obvious. A Web identity helps you promote your business. It can serve as a customer service tool, an employee recruitment vehicle and, obviously, a mechanism to gain new sales/clients.

Random notes:

Make it yours

Recently, a national insurance company decided to change its name. They did market research, brainstorming, group thinks and, in the end, landed on a name everyone was happy with.
The company designed a new logo and redesigned every piece of paper that it used—all its marketing materials, signage—you name it. They spent millions producing all these new pieces. And then they discovered they didn't have the legal right to use the name.

They then spent more than a few thousand dollars on a legal team that tried to win the company the right to use the name. When that didn't work, they re-spent millions on creating an entirely new name and producing all the materials that now needed to be re-branded.

Don't think this could never happen to you. I've had more than one client who discovered that somewhere along the line in the company's past, the legalities of protecting their name were ignored. I don't know if everyone assumes it's such a "duh" that they don't double-check, or if everyone assumes that someone else has it covered. All I know is that it is agonizing and expensive when it does slip through the cracks.

If you're ever involved in a name change or the creation of a new company, be the one to ask the dumb question. You may just save the day.

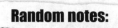
Random notes:

I'm feeling a little ignored

Nearly 70% of business lost in America is lost due to post-sales apathy.

That just stuns me. We spend all this time and effort luring customers to our business. We seduce them on the sales floor. We listen attentively to their problems and help them find solutions. We give them a fair price. We smile and wave as they leave.

And then, we ignore them.

Think about it. On the rare occasion that someone has called, written or emailed you after you bought something to see if you were happy, weren't you surprised? And pleased? I'll bet you also told someone about the phone call. Because it made that much of an impression.

How difficult or time consuming would it be for you to implement a follow-up system? Maybe it's not for every nut or bolt you sell. Perhaps, depending on your business, you set a minimum threshold. It could be based on a dollar amount or volume sold.

But it goes beyond following up on the sale. If you don't have a customer retention program—one that turns your clients into raving fans—you need one. Make it simple, easy to implement and something you will actually do. Consistently. Start on it today. It's that important.

Random notes:

Holidays with a twist

Everyone sends a season's greeting card around Christmastime. It's expected. And your card, along with hundreds of others, gets lost in the shuffle. Unless you do something a little different.

Brackett Media, an innovative media and event services business in the Midwest, created a card that they're still getting talk value from, over a year later. Jay Brackett and his crew dressed up like pilgrims, wearing knee-highs and goofy hats, for their Thanksgiving card photo. Not only did their card beat the holiday rush, but because of the sheer absurdity of the photo, many of their clients kept the card on a bulletin board or wall. Talk about staying top of mind!

If you aren't brave enough to dress like a pilgrim, how about sending a card for a less recognized holiday? When was the last time you got a Groundhog's Day card? Or Labor Day? Or what if you recognized your clients' secretaries on Administrative Professionals Day. Now those would get you noticed!

Or make up your own holiday that is customized for your industry and clients. The point is to have a little fun and do something memorable that shows your clients how much you appreciate their business.

I'm not saying you shouldn't send a Christmas card. It's a very nice thing to do. But because everyone does it, you cannot expect to get much marketing value or even goodwill from it. It's become the norm. And the norm rarely gets noticed.

Random notes:

Your blind spot

This is a touchy subject; so let me handle it delicately. You aren't always right. In fact, dare I say it, sometimes you are dead wrong. Especially if you run your own business.

As an insider, whether you're the VP of Marketing, CEO or owner of the corner deli, you know too much. This is a dangerous place to be because you may assume everyone else knows what you know.

We all make the mistake of not seeing ourselves as others see us. We tend to not see the flaws or kinks in the system. Or perhaps we do see them, but assume our clients don't.

That combination—knowing too much and not seeing ourselves from the customer's point of view—is a train wreck waiting to happen. So how do you avoid the collision? Fortunately, it's easy. Get an outside opinion.

You can do this in several ways. You can hire an agency or consultant. But make sure you hire someone who's a straight shooter. You don't want someone who's afraid to tell you what you don't want to hear. You can also conduct client surveys or focus groups. In either case, the messenger will not only bring you some bad news, but she'll also have insights as to how to solve whatever's causing the problem.

If you are willing to remove the blinders and take an honest look at your business, your blind spot will be gone before you know it.

Random notes:

How far can you stretch?

Everyone wants to do more with less. It's smart business, right? Usually. But sometimes if you stretch too hard, you can hurt yourself. That is certainly the case when it comes to a media budget.

Savvy media buying is a combination of reach (how many people can you get your message to) and frequency (how often will they see/hear the message). If you skimp on either, it can dramatically reduce your effectiveness.

Let's look at a concrete example. A marketing department head might decide she wants to create and run a print ad. But her funds are limited. So, she decides to make a big splash and buys one full-page ad in the *New York Times*. Did she reach a lot of people? You bet. But, will they remember the ad and actually respond to the call to action? In most cases, no. Why not? Because you need the repetition to actually capture and hold reader attention, and to remind them to respond to the call to action.

On the flip side, if a business owner only runs a radio ad on a very niche radio station because it will be played every hour on the hour, he hasn't spent wisely either. Sure, he has plenty of frequency. But he's talking to the same few hundred people over and over again. Only a small percentage of them are even going to be interested in his product or service.

A successful media budget absolutely must give you reach and frequency. Without both, you may be wasting your resources. You can stretch your media budget for sure, but just make sure you know the breaking point.

Random notes:

It takes a chorus

Unless the product or service you sell is incredibly simple, you have at least 3 to 5 key selling points that you believe are compelling to your target audience. You want to communicate each of those selling points in a very clear way, so the potential customer is overcome with desire and need for your product and rushes out to buy it. Right?

You can't accomplish that in a single print ad, radio or TV spot or direct mail piece. We have to stop thinking in terms of creating ads. We need to create campaigns. A campaign, which might consist of 3 direct mail pieces, a bill insert, 2 radio spots and 3 print ads, lets you give each unique selling point its just due. Even if your campaign is a very modest 3 direct mail letters—it's going to be infinitely more successful than a single letter would be.

Each individual piece of the campaign should spotlight one selling point. Can you mention the others? Sure. But the focus and the bulk of the copy should be to capture the benefits of the highlighted feature. Otherwise, you end up summarily listing the reasons why they should buy, which is hardly as persuasive as really exploring a single key reason to buy.

Don't build one superstar ad. Instead build a chorus to sing your ware's praises.

Random notes:

Emily Post was right

No matter what we sell, there are two rather stark realities that we all share. The first—if clients didn't buy our product or service, we would cease to exist. We remain in business because our clients find value in what we do and continue to buy from us. The other reality is, no matter what we sell, someone else sells it too.

Sort of crystallizes how important it is to our survival that our clients choose us, doesn't it?

It only stands to reason that we should say thank you. I'm not talking about the obligatory holiday greeting card or a "thanks" scribbled on an invoice. I am talking honest gratitude that you actually think about and give in a way that is uniquely you.

It doesn't have to be elaborate or expensive. It might be as simple as a phone call or a handwritten note. Maybe you throw a "best clients" party at your place. Some companies give away shirts, jackets or other items with their logo. Or take clients out to dinner or to a ball game. Just be sure it's true to who you are as a company and that it's sincere.

Not only is it good business, it's just good manners.

Random notes:

What is your brand?

Everyone has a brand. It's really just a matter of who gets to decide what it is. Nature hates a vacuum. So if you don't create and nurture a brand for your company, your consumers will.

At our company, we have a patented process we call the Handshake™. It takes a client on an exploration that results in a branding statement that is truly unique, fresh and most important—true.

Too many companies confuse the idea of their brand with their "tagline of the month." A brand is timeless. It's not something you change on a whim. It comes from the soul of your company.

Not sure if you have a brand or what it might be? Poll your employees to find out what they're hearing your customers say. Or go directly to your customers and ask them to describe your company in a word or phrase. See a consistency or trend? If so, you have just identified what, in your consumers' minds anyway, is your most compelling attribute. Unless you tell them something different—it will become your brand.

Is it accurate? Does it separate you from your competitors? Is it how you want to be perceived?

Random notes:

www.tunes.com

It's natural to want your URL to match your company name. That's just how it's usually done. You don't see Tide® using www.stinkbegone.com or Chevrolet® advertising www.walknomore.com. In most cases, URLs are pretty straightforward.

But there may be an opportunity missed by doing what everyone else does. Imagine a bank using www.moola.com or a car company using www.zoom-zoom.com. What would that tell you about them and their brand? How does your reaction to the company differ from how you respond to the more expected www.bankofamerica.com or www.ford.com?

If you're trying to set yourself apart from your competition, this might be an easy way to really cement your brand. Brainstorm a word or phrase (if you don't already have one) that captures your brand, and then go to www.networksolutions.com to see if the URL is available.

If this makes you a little nervous, you can also register your company name as a URL and then no matter which one people type in—they'll get to your Web page. If you find that your company name is already being used as someone else's URL, consider the brand word URL as your primary URL.

Want proof that this is a strong branding strategy? Visit www.tunes.com and see how right on the money it is.

Random notes:

Be precise

Details give a story richness and meaning. The same is true of marketing copy. If you were to read a press release that talked about a rally where many people stormed the capital to protest a new law, how many people would you envision? 20? 100? 1,000? How about hearing about a new-fangled widget that has several patents. Would you imagine 3 patents? 10? 26?

All too often, we use generalities in our marketing materials. It's safe. And it's easier. You don't have to dig up the details. Sometimes you are tight on space. But it is costing you money and credibility.

One of the best ways to reassure a potential client that you aren't all hype is to document your claims with facts and details. There is something much more believable about 7 patents than the generic several. An actual testimonial saying, "The pie is so good it's indescribable! If I didn't think my husband and kids would be embarrassed, I'd lick the plate!" is far more powerful than copy that says, "Our customers rave about our pie."

Read over your marketing materials. Look for generalities or vague references that could be edited to add color, depth and authenticity to your efforts.

Random notes:

Be the expert

If you run a service business or provide consulting services, you dispense knowledge every day. There's a way to harness that knowledge and use it for your marketing purposes. And all you have to do is the same thing you do everyday.

Most communities have a least one talk radio station in their midst. Most of them are a mix of local and national syndicated programming. Your goal—to get on the radio and talk about your field of expertise. What a magnificent way to let a wide variety of potential customers sample your expertise and style. Here are a couple different ways to go about it.

- If your schedule would make a regular commitment possible, talk to the programming director about hosting a weekly call-in show related to your field. For two hours every week, you'd be giving potential customers a sample of how you work and think.

- If two hours every week isn't doable, talk to them about being a substitute host. There are going to be times when the regular on-air personalities can't be there. You'd probably be even more valuable to them if you were available for emergencies.

- Find out how the station books guests for their regular local programming. Figure out where you'd fit best and get scheduled. If the segment goes well, they'll probably keep asking you back. It might even develop into a more regular gig.

There is a built-in credibility to an objective third party, like a radio station that positions you as an expert. Find a way to take advantage of that powerful positioning.

Random notes:

Did you Google™ him?

With the Internet has come a whole new language filled with acronyms, jargon and completely new words, like "Google." Here are some Internet-inspired terms that marketers should know.

- **Bandwidth:** How much data you can send through a connection. Usually measured in bits-per-second. A full page of English text is about 16,000 bits. A fast modem can move about 57,000 bits in one second. Full-motion full-screen video would require roughly 10,000,000 bits-per-second. This is critical information as you design and build Web pages or plan on sending data and images via the Internet.

- **Blog (weB LOG):** A blog is basically a journal that is available on the Web. The activity of updating a blog is called blogging, and a blogger is someone who keeps a blog. You can find a blog on just about any topic you can imagine.

- **Portal:** A Web site that is created to be the first place people see when using the Web. Typically a portal site has a catalog of Web sites and/or a search engine. A portal site may also offer email and other services to entice people to use that site as their main point of entry to the Web. Yahoo® would be a good example.

It only makes sense that something that has completely altered the way we work, play and interact would also change the way we talk. If you haven't been using these terms, you soon will be.

Random notes:

Can I ask you a question?

Even the most poised public speaker gets a little sweaty palmed at the notion of the Q&A portion of the speech. You can practice your presentation, but you are flying without a net when it comes to open mic time. You can reduce your anxiety by prepping for the difficult questions in advance.

Take the time to anticipate the tough questions. Think about the concerns that might be brewing and what queries might rise from them. Then, make a list of all possible questions and positive points or facts for each.

Don't think you need to sugar coat things though. If you are tossed a fireball and the truth isn't pretty, gently and respectfully deliver the truth. You'll earn the audience's respect, even if they don't like the answer. If you try to give them a fluff answer, they'll smell a cover-up or dodge immediately, and you'll never get a second chance.

Another way to ease the Q&A session is to ask people to submit their questions in writing. The questions themselves won't necessarily be any easier, but since you get to read them out loud, much of the sting of a harsh delivery will be taken away. Make sure you read them exactly as they were written though, even if the grammar or language is a little rough. This too will buy you credibility.

It's never easy to be in the hot seat, but when handled with grace and truthfulness, you'll come off as being both confident and approachable.

Random notes:

A storm's a brewin'

Brainstorming meetings can be a very effective way to generate new ideas, explore current practices and plan for the future. But, because of their free-for-all nature, they can also get off track in a hurry. Here are some guidelines for keeping everyone focused and productive.

- Hand out a brief on your issue or goal prior to the meeting so everyone can let the ideas percolate for a few days before coming together.

- Invite new employees or employees who have a different perspective on the problem. They'll bring a fresh point of view to the process.

- Do not invite the entire company. The ideal size for a brainstorming meeting is 4 to 10 people. Enough energy and divergent ideas to keep things hopping, but not so many voices that everyone gets bogged down in the process.

- No critiquing. This is not the meeting to decide if an idea is feasible or affordable. The craziest of ideas might spark another thought or avenue to explore.

- Hold the meeting when everyone's energy is high. Don't call a brainstorming meeting right after lunch or at the very end of the day. Get your participants when they're fresh and full of energy.

Implement these practical steps and pretty soon you'll be whipping up a storm!

Random notes:

Reach out and grab them!

Print advertising has been a staple of most marketing efforts for years. Whether they're in a traditional print medium or online, print ads are here to stay. One of the most critical elements of any print ad is the headline. That's one of your biggest hooks. If the headline doesn't grab your readers, you're starting to sink. So what works well?

- Headlines that identify with the ad's audience: "You don't have to worry about his mother any more!" (A headline that will catch the attention of almost every wife!)

- Cut right to the benefit: "The best seats for the hottest concerts. The only downside? You'll never have to wait in an overnight line again!"

- There's a lot to be said for a concise headline. Look at the Absolut Vodka® campaign. But long headlines are not absolutely taboo. Toro® did some research on their print ads and found that headlines with 20+ words sold 20% better than their shorter counterparts. If you need the extra words to make your point—use them.

The headline is only the beginning of a potent print ad. But if you start off weak, it's tough to earn back their attention. So come out strong and hook them from the very first word.

Random notes:

Two-timing will cut your media exposure in no time

If you have a story to pitch to the media, choose the reporter or media outlet that is best suited for the story. But don't pitch the same story to competing media or more than one reporter at the same place. That will kill you.

Even if you get coverage of the story in two places, the price you'll pay in terms of your credibility is not worth it. And the next time you pick up the phone with a hot lead—the reporter you burned will never bother returning your call. He probably caught a lot of heat from the news director or editor for running the same story as the competition and is not about to let you do that again.

If you have a big story or event that has enough appeal that everyone will want to cover it, that's fine. But be clear with all of them that this is not exclusive information and play fair. Everyone gets the same press packet or release.

The best marketing professionals understand they need to cultivate relationships with the reporters that cover their industry. Making that reporter look foolish is hardly going to strengthen the relationship. Or improve your chances of getting another story placed.

Random notes:

Leave them wanting more

Think of your ongoing conversation with your potential customer as though you were a romantic suitor. The art of courting someone is taking your time and enjoying the natural give and take. You don't sit down on a first date and tell the other person every single fact about you and your life. They're not ready to receive all of that information.

Your prospect is the same way. You cannot inundate them with every

Index

Random notes:

Random notes:

Drew McLellan has not only survived 20 years in the advertising and marketing arena, he's thrived in it. After working for several other agencies, including Young and Rubicam's CMF&Z, Drew and his business partner created Erickson • McLellan in 1995. With tongue firmly in cheek, they refer to themselves as the uptight, straight-laced marketing professionals as they bring their passion and practical smarts to life for their clients small and large.

Drew is highly sought after and has given countless presentations on marketing to his peers in the profession, college students and even his daughter's fourth grade class. What's so appealing about Drew that he can reach such a diverse audience? He's a straight shooter who talks about marketing in a way you won't forget. He tells stories and gives you concrete examples and facts that you can take into the boardroom. Most importantly, his ideas work, no matter who you are or what your level of experience.

Over the years, Drew has lent his expertise to clients like Nabisco, IAMS, Kraft Foods, Meredith Publishing, John Deere, Iowa Health System, Make-A-Wish, University of Central Florida, SkiDoo and a wide array of others. When he's not out preaching the good word of marketing, Drew spends time with his family and pondering why the Dodgers can't seem to get back to the World Series.

Visit www.randomactsofmarketing.com to take advantage of some free marketing tools or write to Drew at drew@randomactsofmarketing.com